EMPEROR PENGUIN

SENSATIONAL SURVIVOR

PAIGE V. POLINSKY

CONSULTING EDITOR, DIANE CRAIG, M.A./READING SPECIALIST

Super Sandcastle

An Imprint of Abdo Publishing
abdopublishing.com

abdopublishing.com

Published by Abdo Publishing, a division of ABDO, PO Box 398166, Minneapolis, Minnesota 55439. Copyright © 2017 by Abdo Consulting Group, Inc. International copyrights reserved in all countries. No part of this book may be reproduced in any form without written permission from the publisher. Super SandCastle™ is a trademark and logo of Abdo Publishing.

Printed in the United States of America, North Mankato, Minnesota
062016
092016

THIS BOOK CONTAINS RECYCLED MATERIALS

Editor: Rebecca Felix
Content Developer: Nancy Tuminelly
Cover and Interior Design and Production: Christa Schneider, Mighty Media, Inc.
Photo Credits: iStockphoto; Mighty Media, Inc.; Minden Pictures/SuperStock; Norbert Wu/Minden Pictures; Shutterstock

Library of Congress Cataloging-in-Publication Data

Names: Polinsky, Paige V., author.
Title: Emperor penguin : sensational survivor / by Paige V. Polinsky.
Description: Minneapolis, Minnesota : Abdo Publishing, [2017] | Series:
   Animal superstars
Identifiers: LCCN 2016006316 (print) | LCCN 2016007039 (ebook) | ISBN
   9781680781489 (print) | ISBN 9781680775914 (ebook)
Subjects: LCSH: Emperor penguin--Juvenile literature. | Penguins--Juvenile
   literature.
Classification: LCC QL696.S473 P65 2016 (print) | LCC QL696.S473 (ebook) |
   DDC 598.47--dc23
LC record available at http://lccn.loc.gov/2016006316

Super SandCastle™ books are created by a team of professional educators, reading specialists, and content developers around five essential components— phonemic awareness, phonics, vocabulary, text comprehension, and fluency—to assist young readers as they develop reading skills and strategies and increase their general knowledge. All books are written, reviewed, and leveled for guided reading, early reading intervention, and Accelerated Reader™ programs for use in shared, guided, and independent reading and writing activities to support a balanced approach to literacy instruction.

CONTENTS

BIG BIRDS

There are 18 types of penguins. Emperor penguins are the largest. They weigh more than 80 pounds (40 kg). They are about 45 inches (115 cm) tall.

45 INCHES (115 CM)

AN ADULT EMPEROR PENGUIN IS AS TALL AS AN AVERAGE SIX-YEAR-OLD CHILD.

BITTER COLD

Emperor penguins live in Antarctica. It is the world's coldest continent.

ANTARCTICA

SOUTH POLE

MAP KEY

● = WHERE EMPEROR PENGUINS LIVE

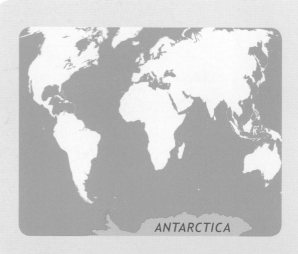

ANTARCTICA

There is no shelter from Antarctica's icy wind.

STRONG SURVIVORS

Only superstars can survive such cold weather! Emperor penguins **huddle** together. This keeps them warm.

Emperor penguins also have **blubber** under their skin. It keeps them warm too.

9

FLUFFY FEATHERS

Emperor penguins are black, white, and yellow. Their feathers are **waterproof**. Emperor penguins lose their feathers each year. New feathers take their place. This is called molting.

DEEP DIVERS

Emperor penguins cannot fly. But they are great swimmers. Their wings act as paddles. They dive deeper than any other bird. And they can hold their breath for up to 22 minutes!

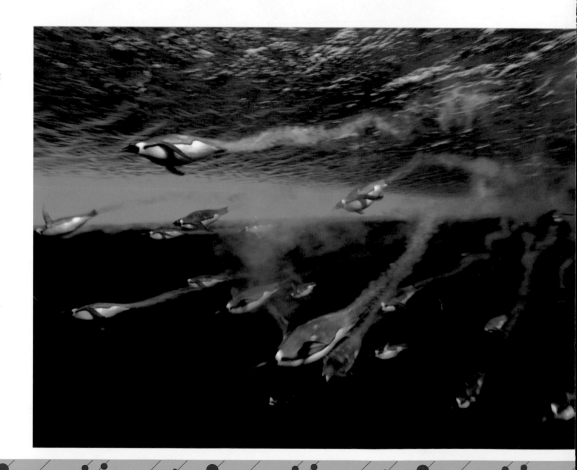

DEEP-SEA DIVING

1,854 FEET
(565 M)
DEEPEST
RECORDED
EMPEROR
PENGUIN DIVE

656 FEET
(200 M)
AVERAGE
EMPEROR
PENGUIN DIVE

331 FEET
(101 M)
DEEPEST
UNASSISTED
HUMAN DIVE

FISH FEASTS

Emperor penguins eat fish. They also eat squid and **krill**. It takes speed to catch these meals! Emperor penguins can swim up to 6 miles per hour (10 kmh).

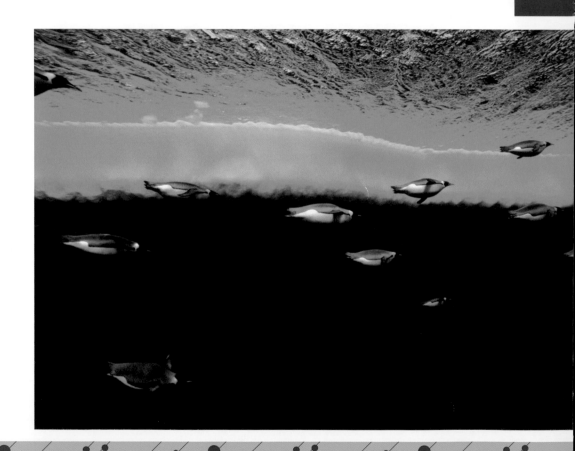

BUBBLE BOOST

EMPEROR PENGUINS EXIT THE SEA AT TOP SPEEDS. TO DO THIS, THEY SHOOT STREAMS OF BUBBLES FROM THEIR FEATHERS.

MOMS ON A MISSION

In the winter, female emperor penguins each lay one egg. They then walk to the ocean. This can be up to 50 miles (80 km) away.

Mother penguins store food that they catch. They later feed it to their chicks.

DEVOTED DADS

Male emperor penguins stay behind while the females hunt. They care for the eggs. They keep the chicks warm once they hatch. The males do not eat until the females return. This takes two months.

FULL OF FATHERS

COULMAN ISLAND IS HOME TO 25,000 MALE EMPEROR PENGUINS.

ICE ISSUE

Global warming is melting sea ice. Emperor penguins' home is **shrinking**. **Krill** need sea ice to survive too. Less ice means less penguin food. Scientists think emperor penguins may become **endangered**.

PENGUIN SUPERSTAR

Can you imagine an
emperor penguin
superstar?
What **awards**
would it win?

WHAT DO YOU KNOW ABOUT
EMPEROR PENGUINS?

1. Emperor penguins **huddle** together to stay warm.

True or false?

2. An emperor penguin loses its feathers each year.

True or false?

3. Emperor penguins are very slow swimmers.

True or false?

4. A mother emperor penguin lays two eggs.

True or false?

ANSWERS:
1. TRUE 2. TRUE 3. FALSE 4. FALSE

GLOSSARY

AWARD - a prize.

BLUBBER - the fat on the bodies of large sea mammals such as dolphins and penguins.

ENDANGERED - having few of a type of plant or animal left in the world.

GLOBAL WARMING - an increase in the average temperature of Earth's surface.

HUDDLE - to crowd, push, or pile together.

KRILL - very small creatures that live in the ocean.

SHRINK - to become smaller.

WATERPROOF - made to keep water out.